If I Ascend To Heaven
You Are There

Psalm 139:8

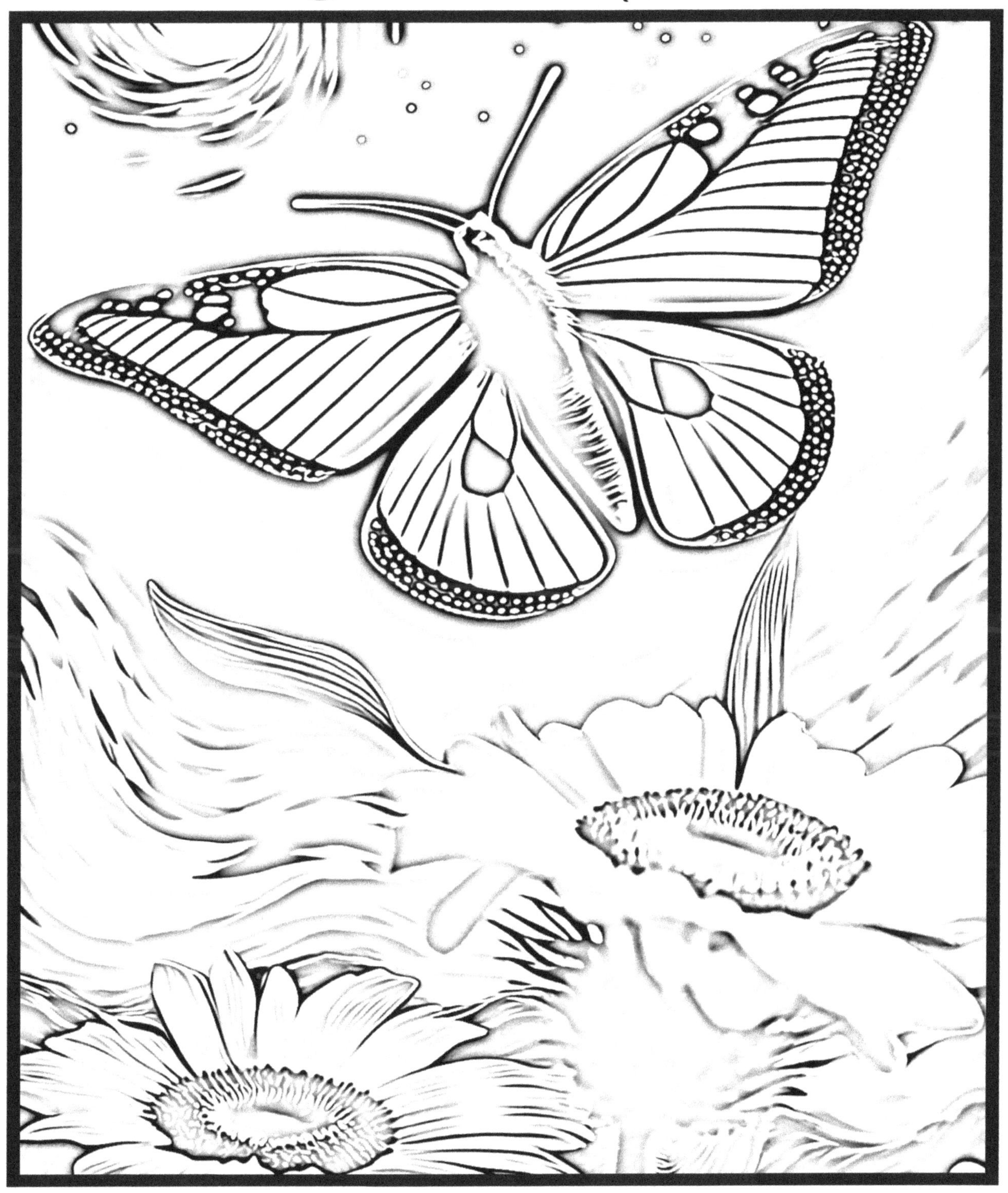

If I Descend To The Depths, You Are There

Psalm 139:8

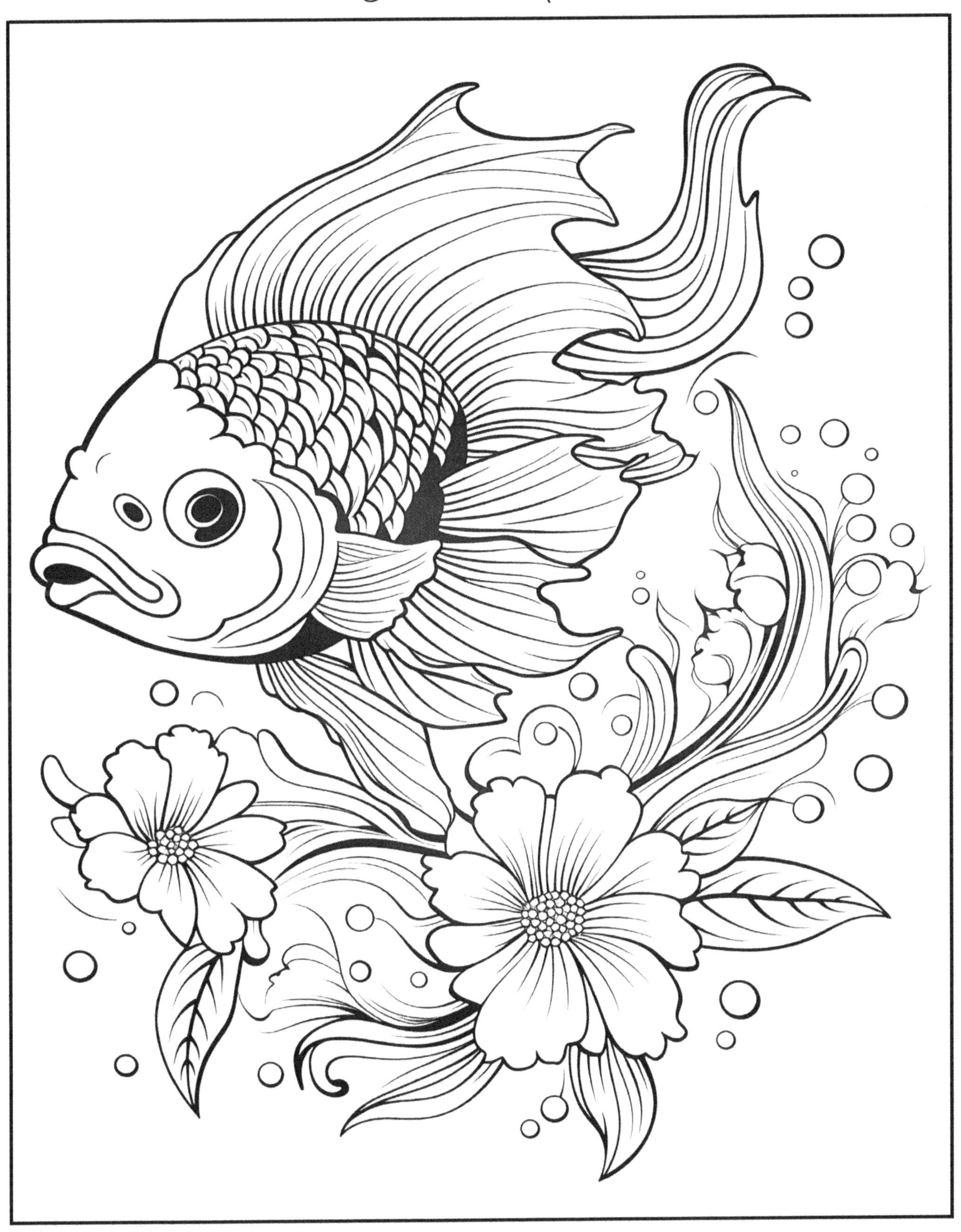

The Lord Is My Shepherd, I Shall Not Want

Psalm 23

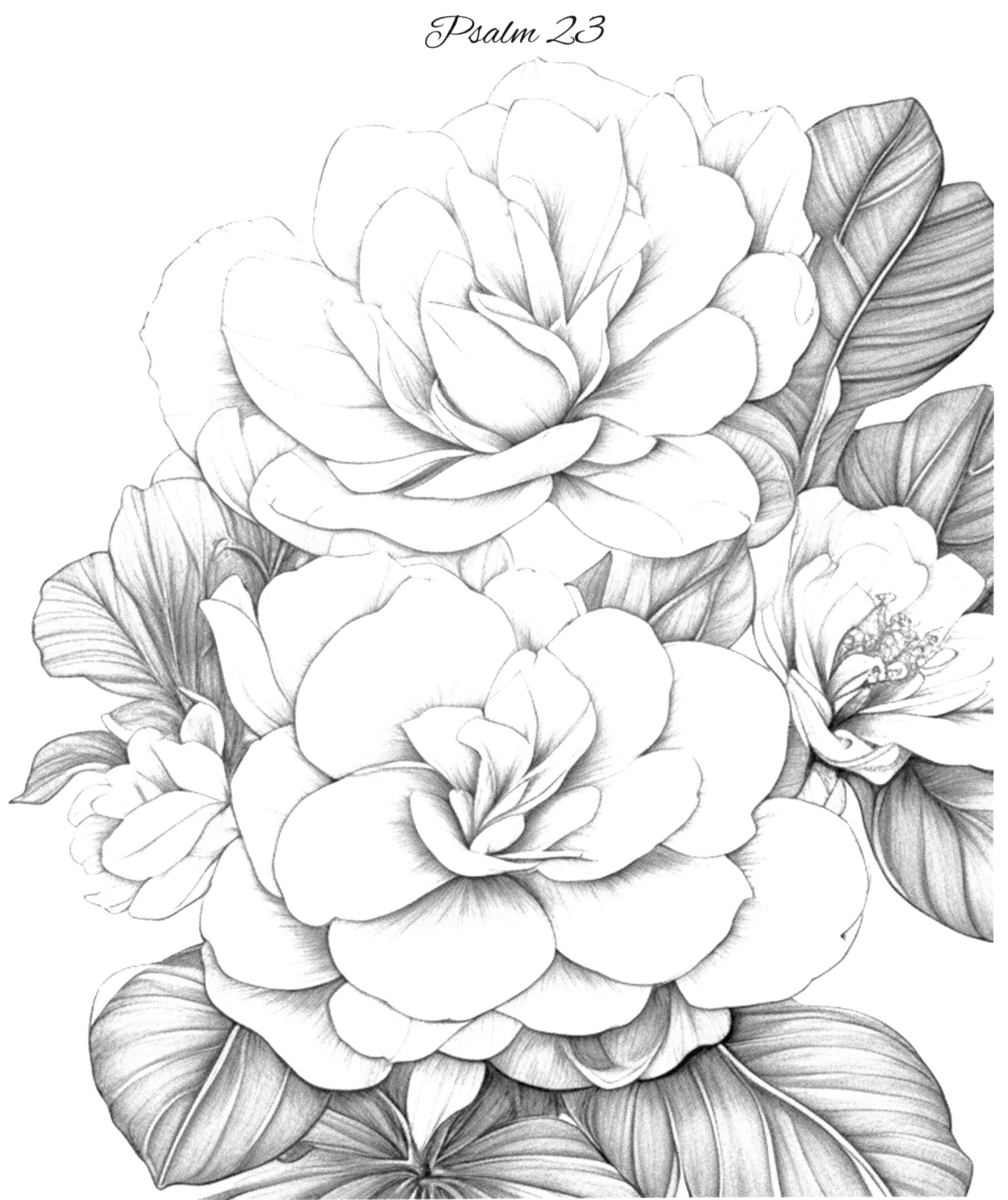

Let The Weak Say
I Am Strong
Joel 3:10

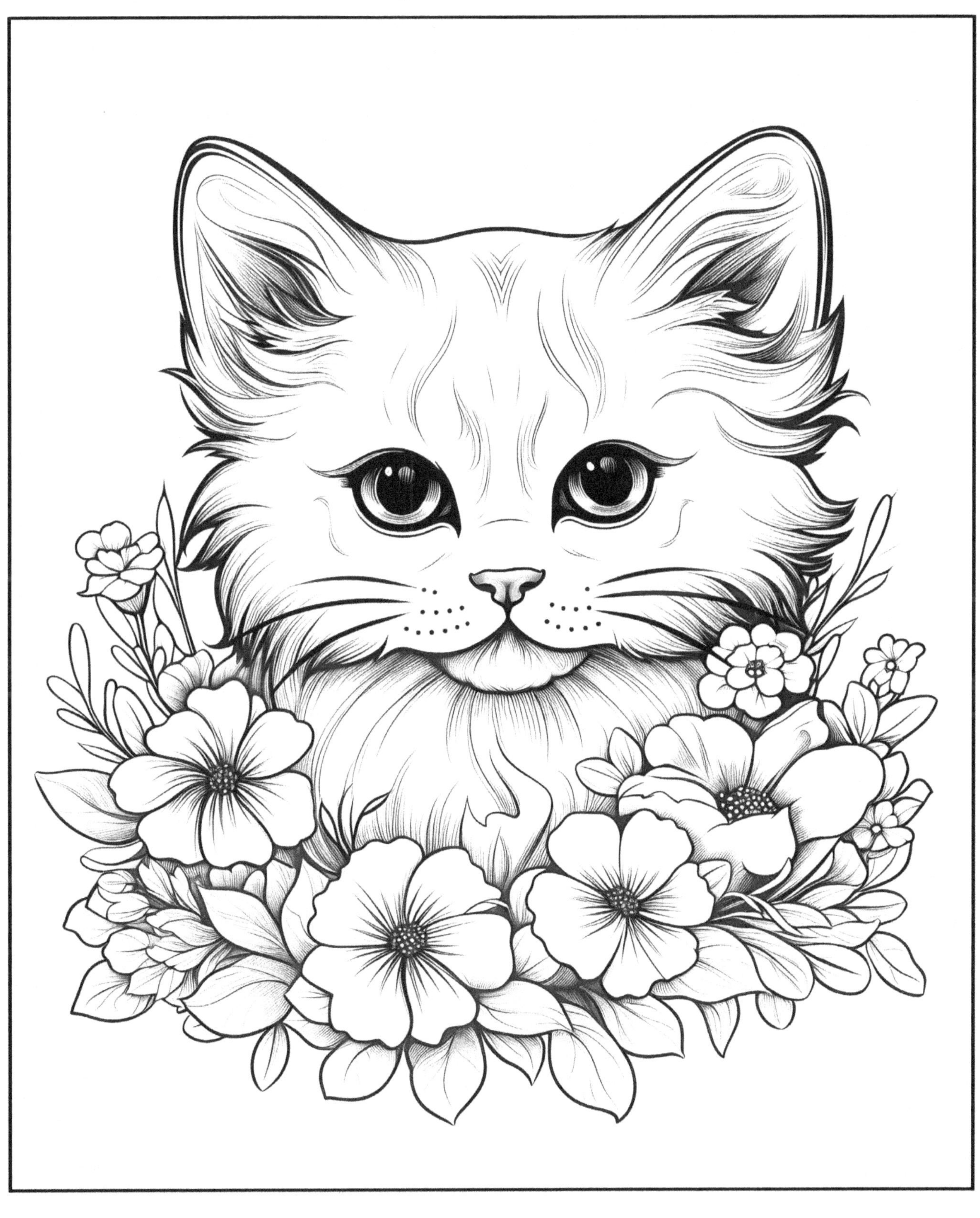

It Is The Lord Your God Who Fights For You

Deuteronomy 3:22

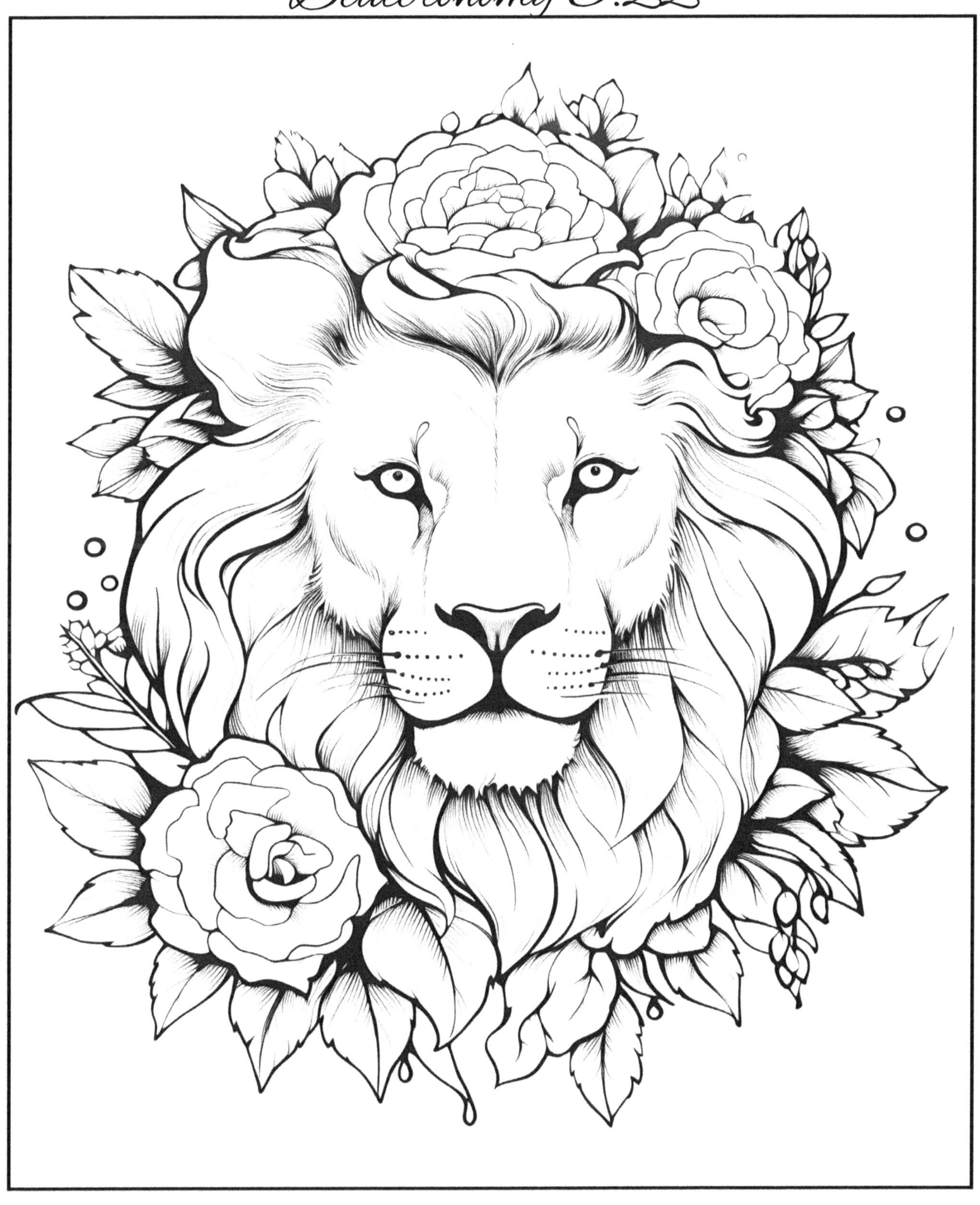

Faith, Hope and Love

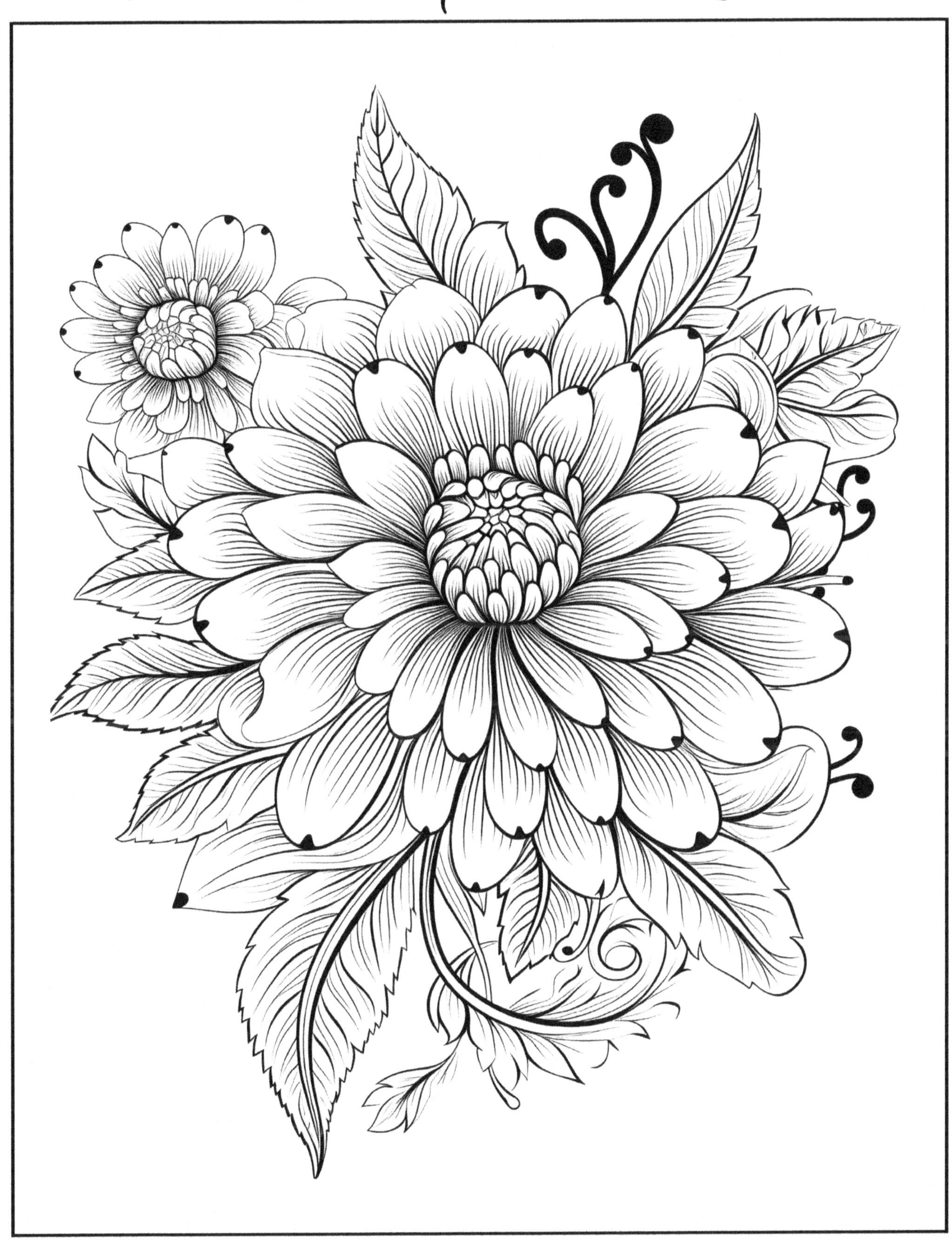

Don't Be Anxious For anything, But By Prayer and Thanksgiving Present Your Requests To God

Pillippians 4:6

Give And It Will Be Given Unto You

Luke 6:38

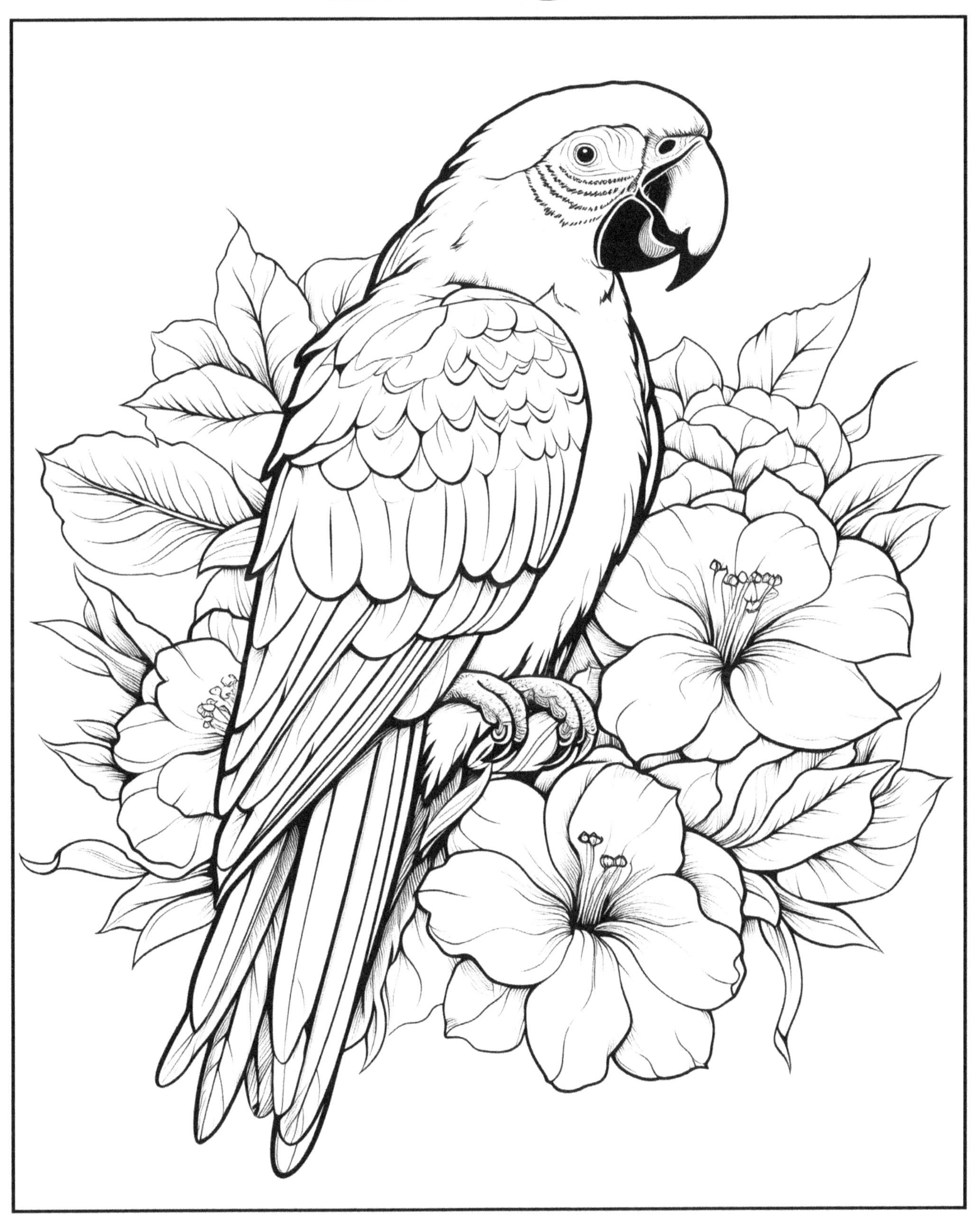

The Lord Make His Face Shine On You And Be Gracious To You

Numbers 6:25

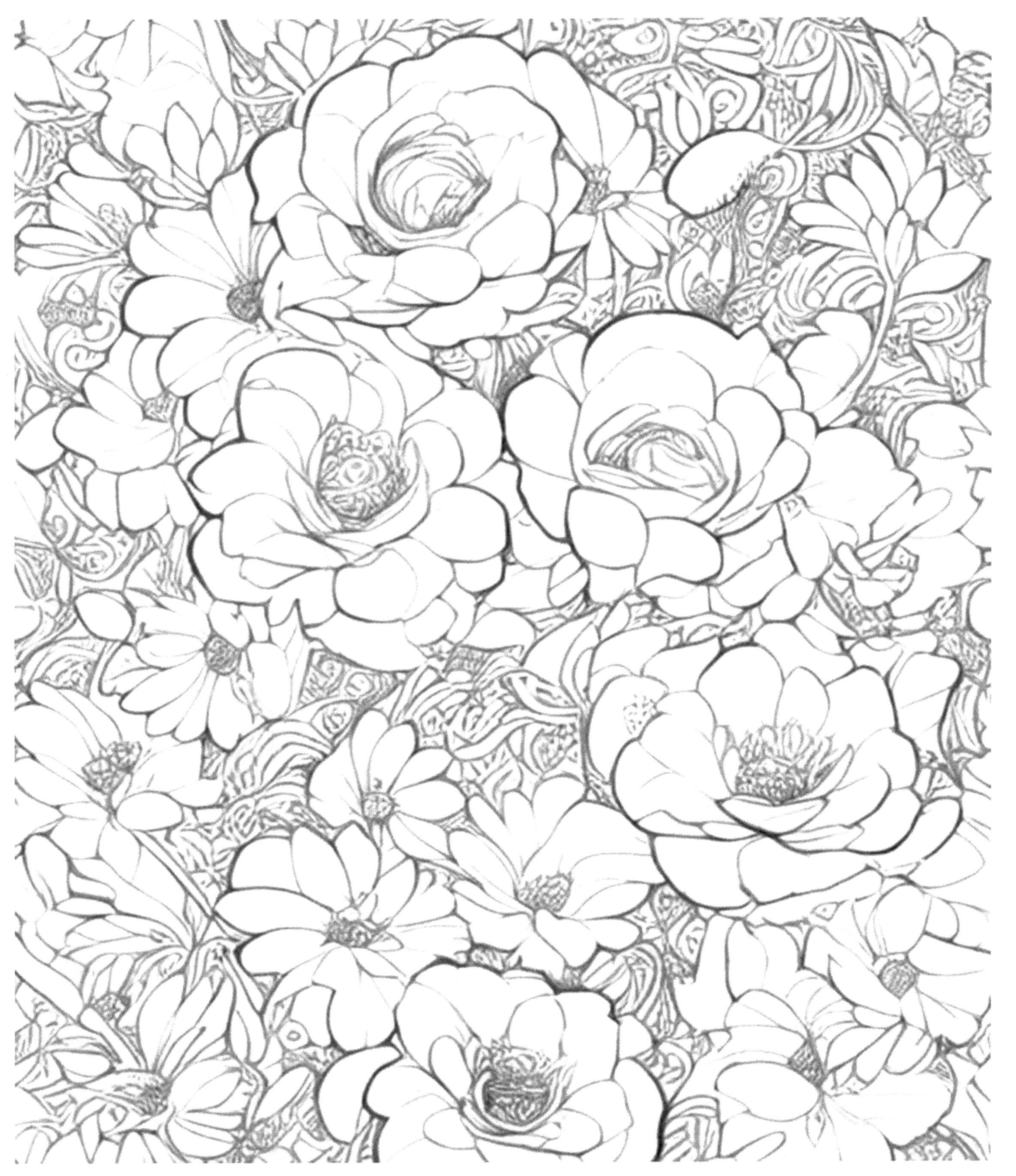

*Seek First The Kingdom
Of God And Everything Else Will
Be Given Unto You*

Matthew 6:33

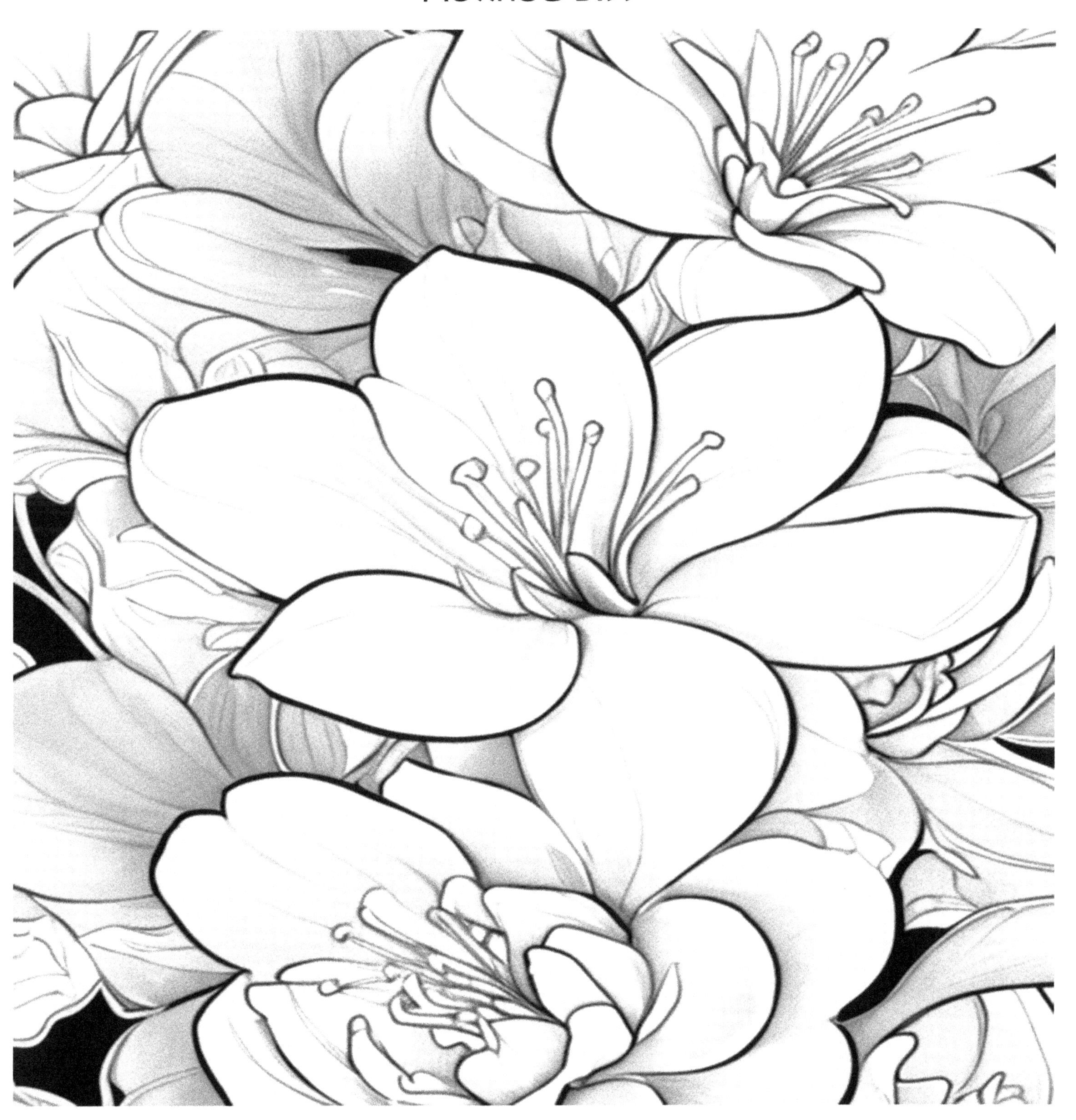

Love Your Enemies

Matthew 5:44

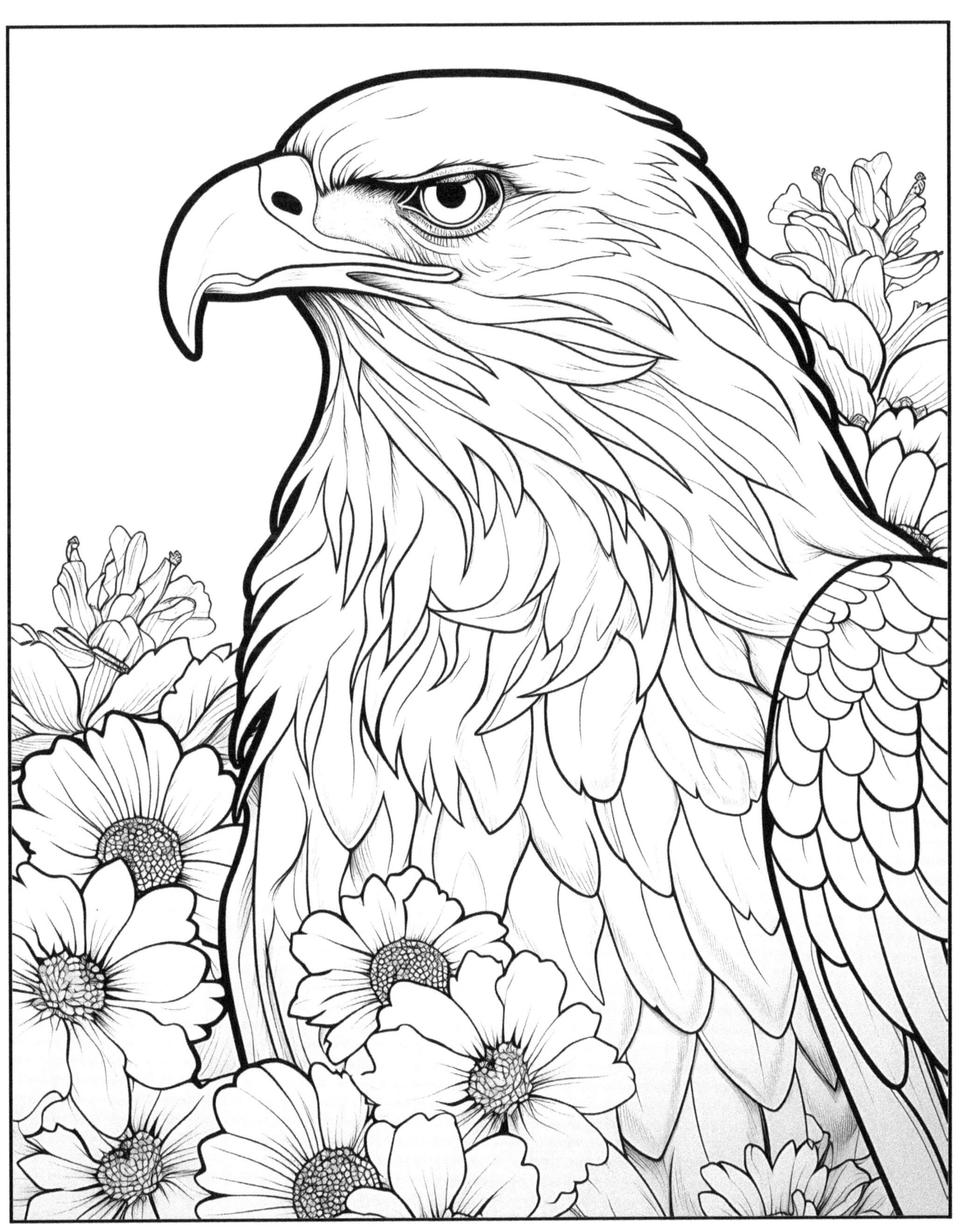

If God Cares For The Wildflowers, He Will Certainly Care For You

Matthew 6:30

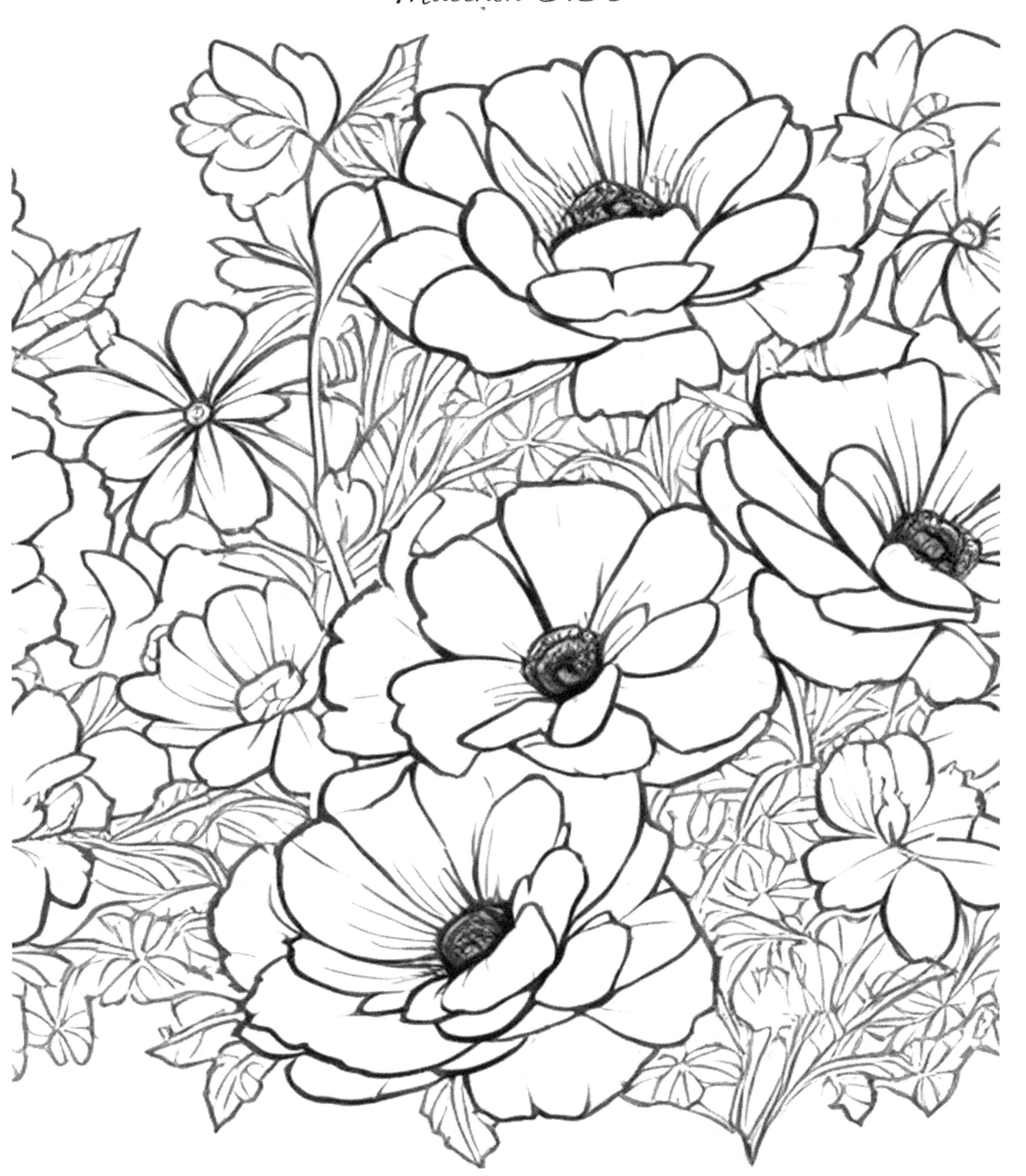

Delight Yourself In The Lord And He Will Give You The Desires Of Your Heart

Psalm 37:4

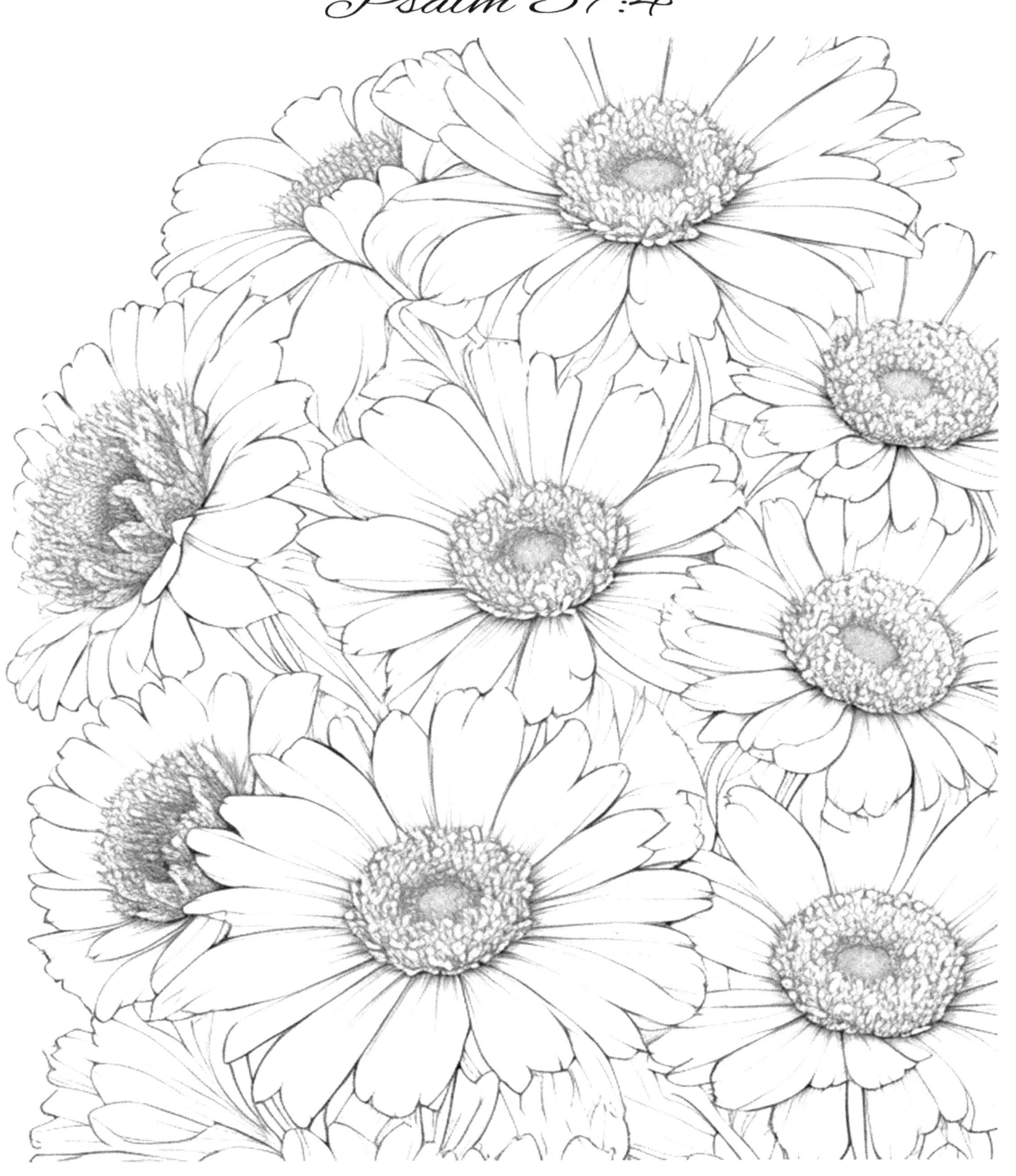

As For Me, I Will Always Have Hope

Psalm 71:14

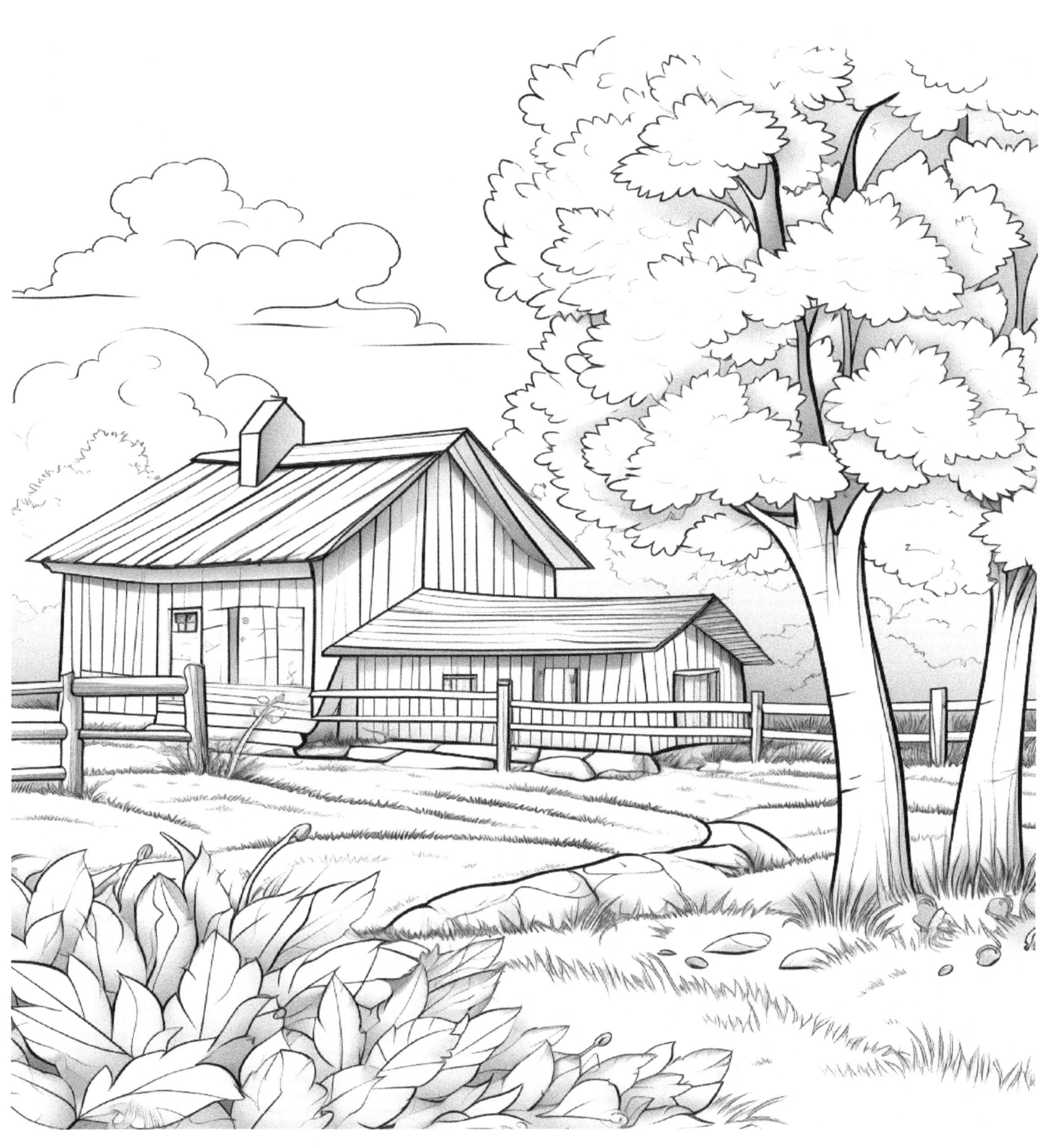

He Will Call upon Me And I Will Answer Him

Psalm 91:15

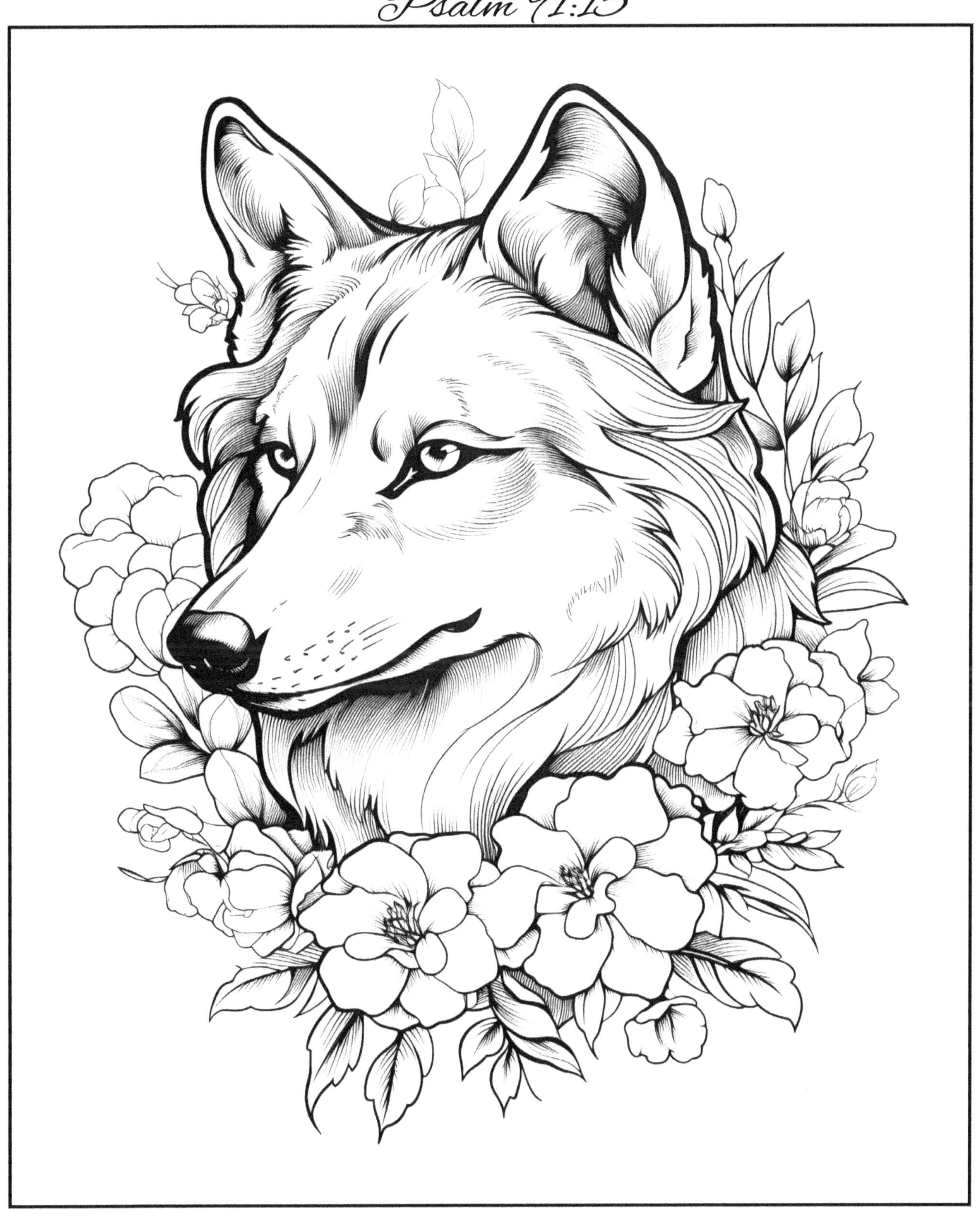

Do Not Let Your Hearts Be Troubled

John 14:1

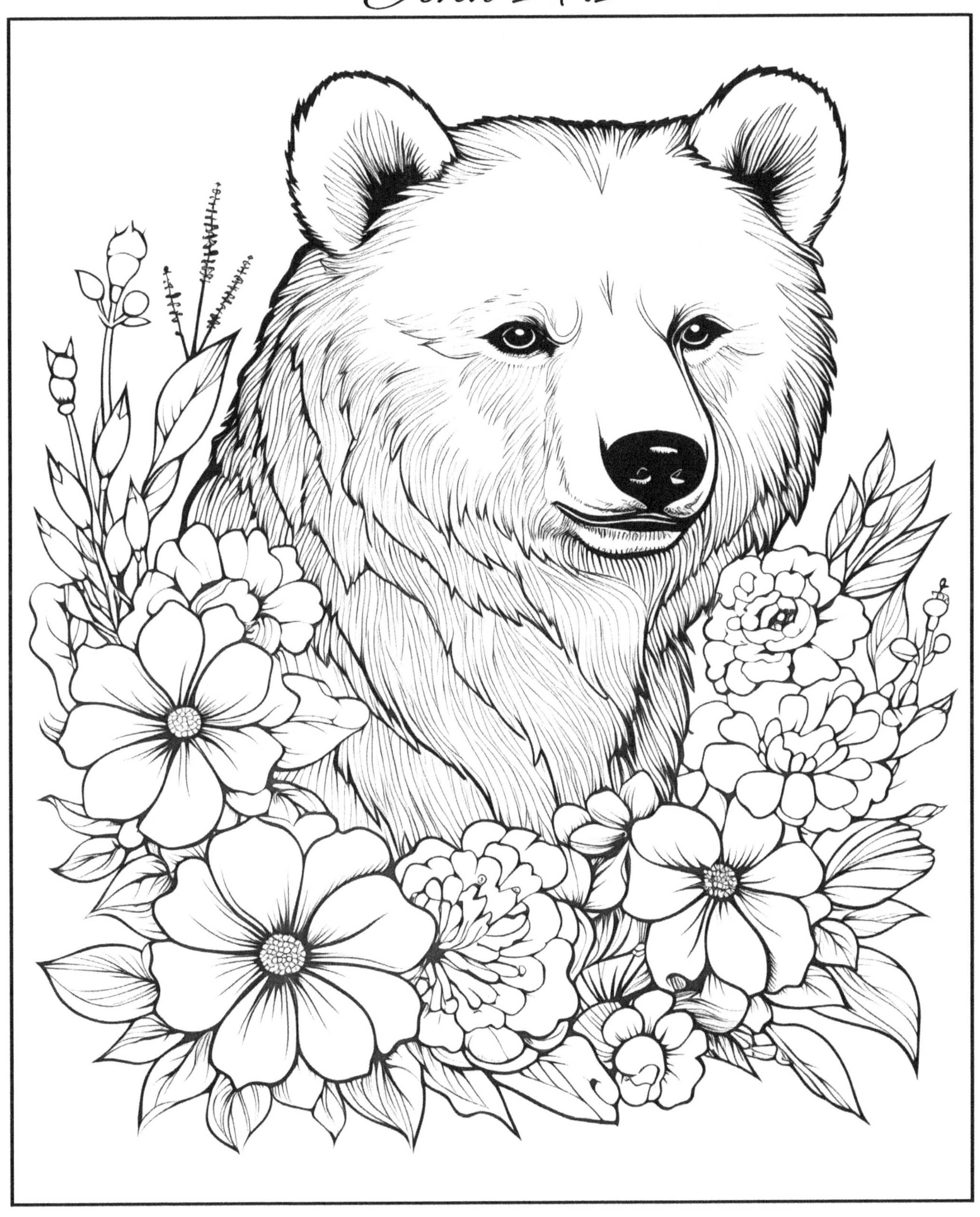

I Have Loved You With An Everlasting Love

Jeremiah 31:3

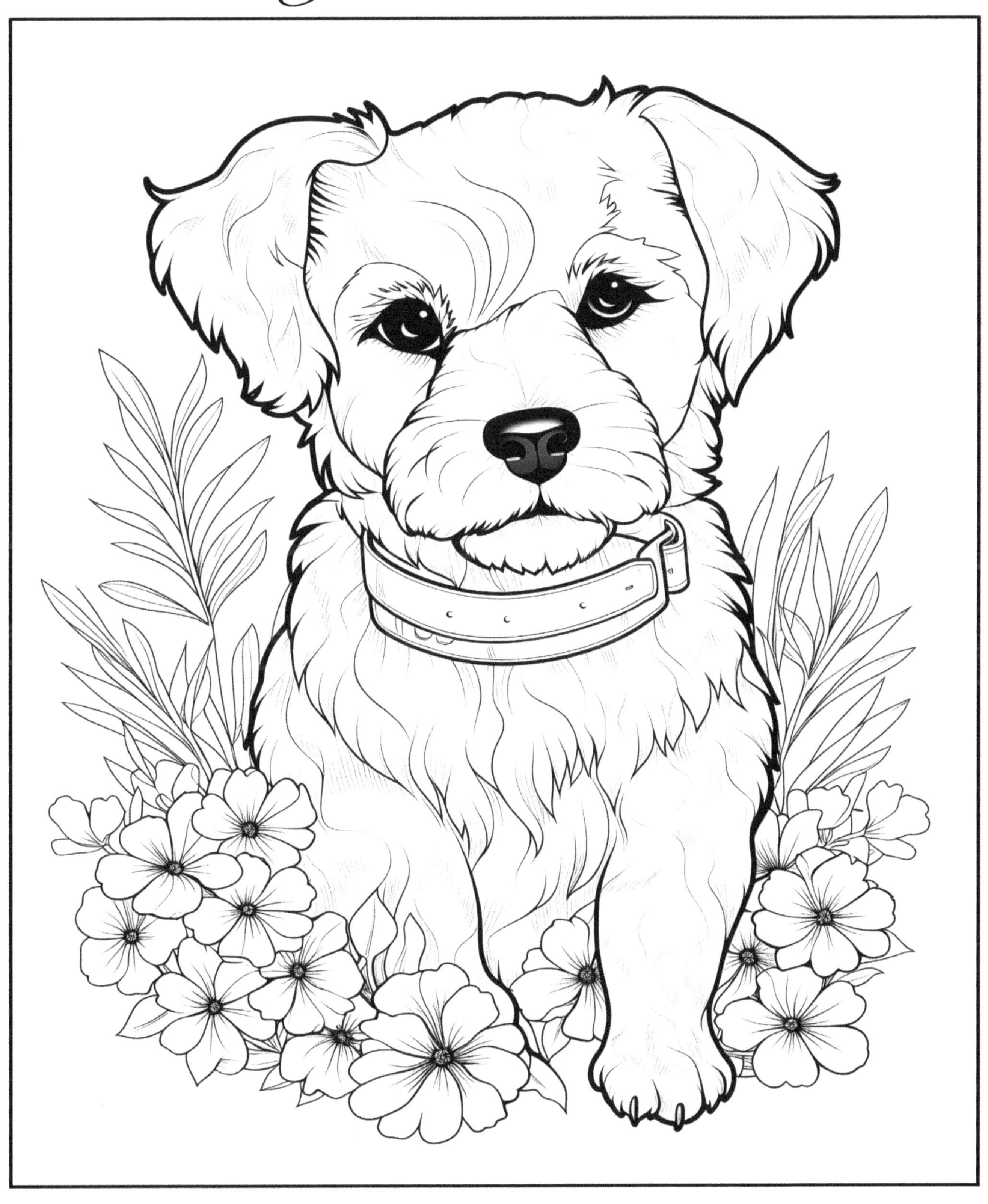

God is Our Refuge
And Strength
Psalm 46:1

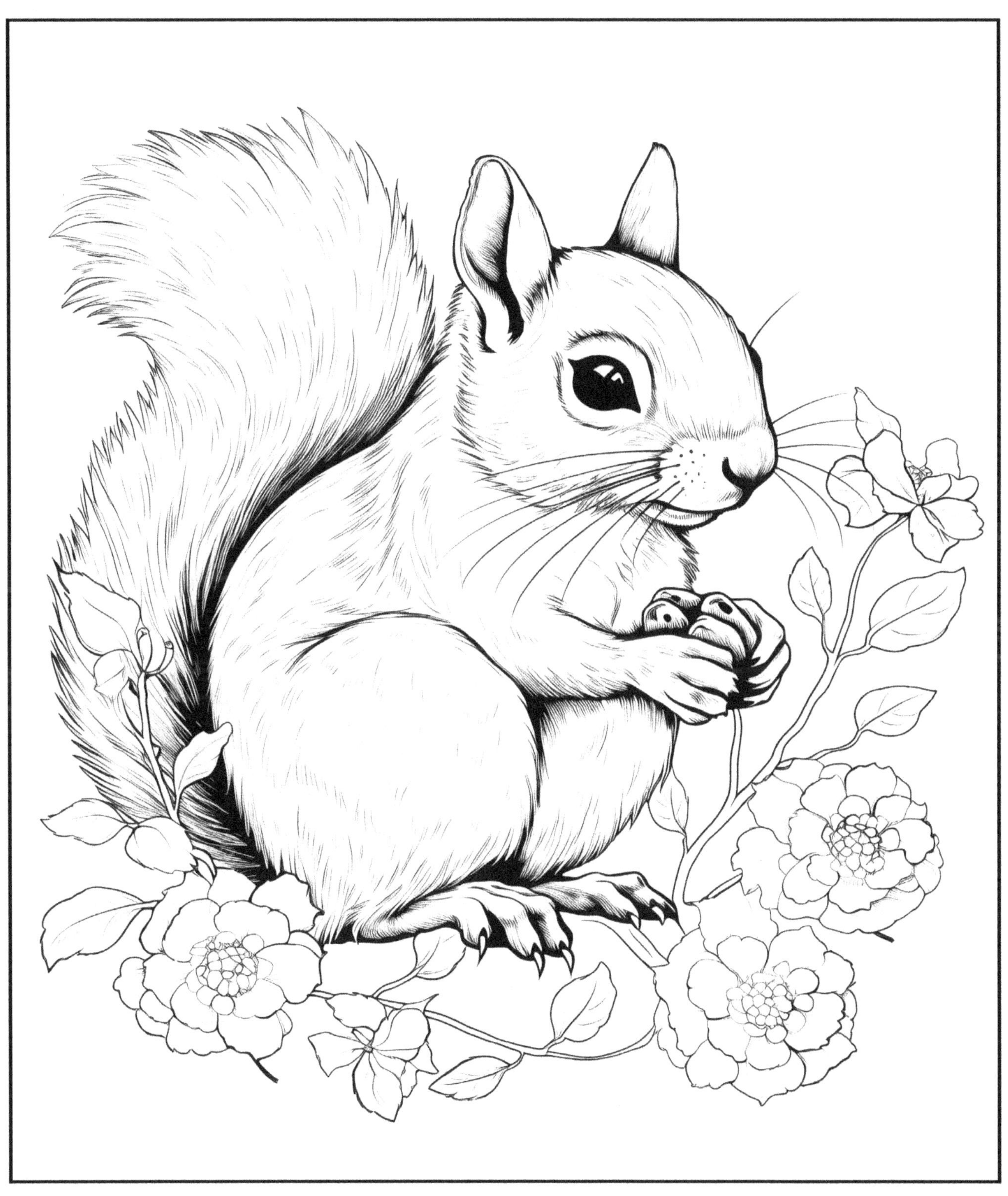

God Is Love

1 John 4:16

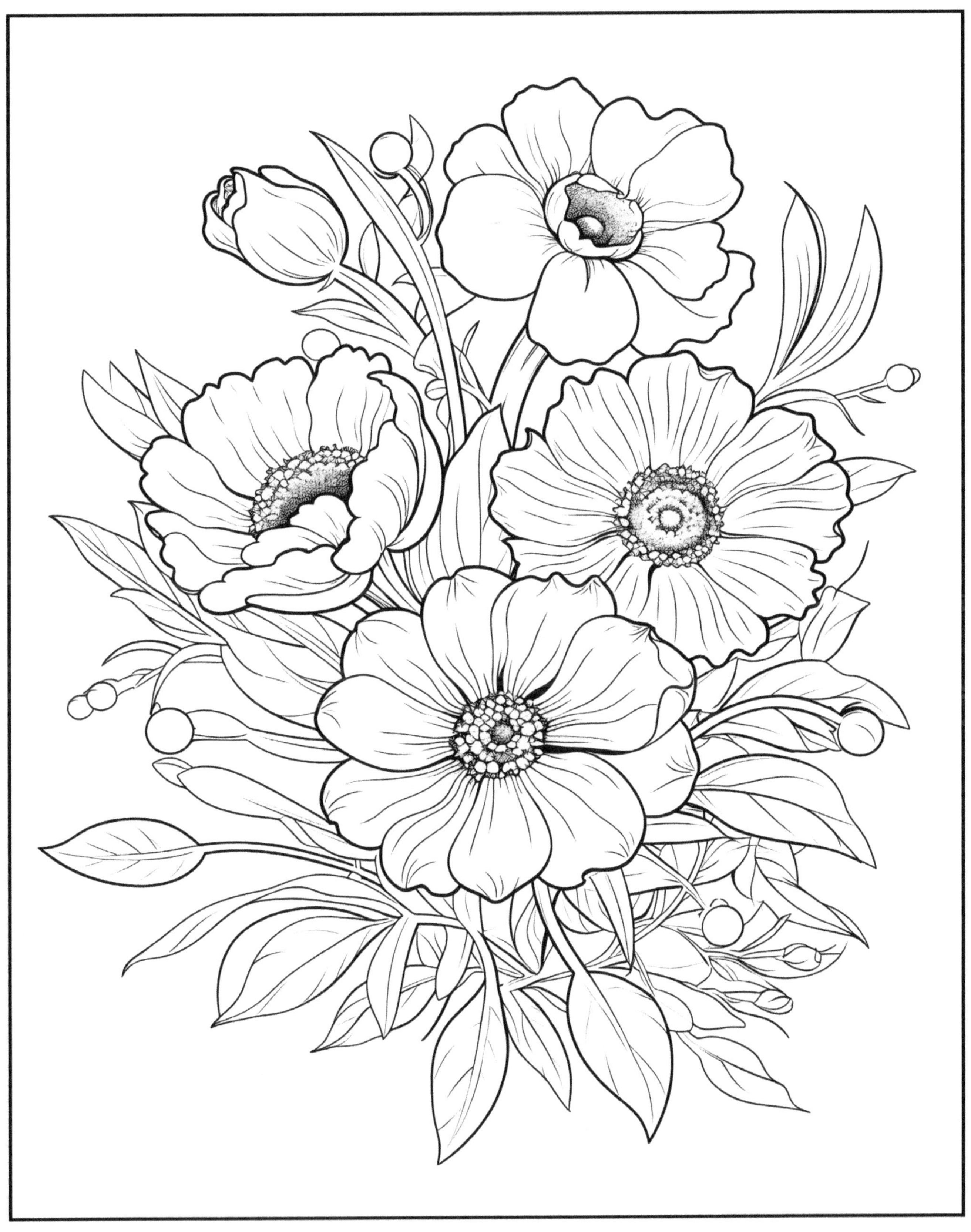

Jesus Said "I Am The Way The Truth And The Life"

John 14:6

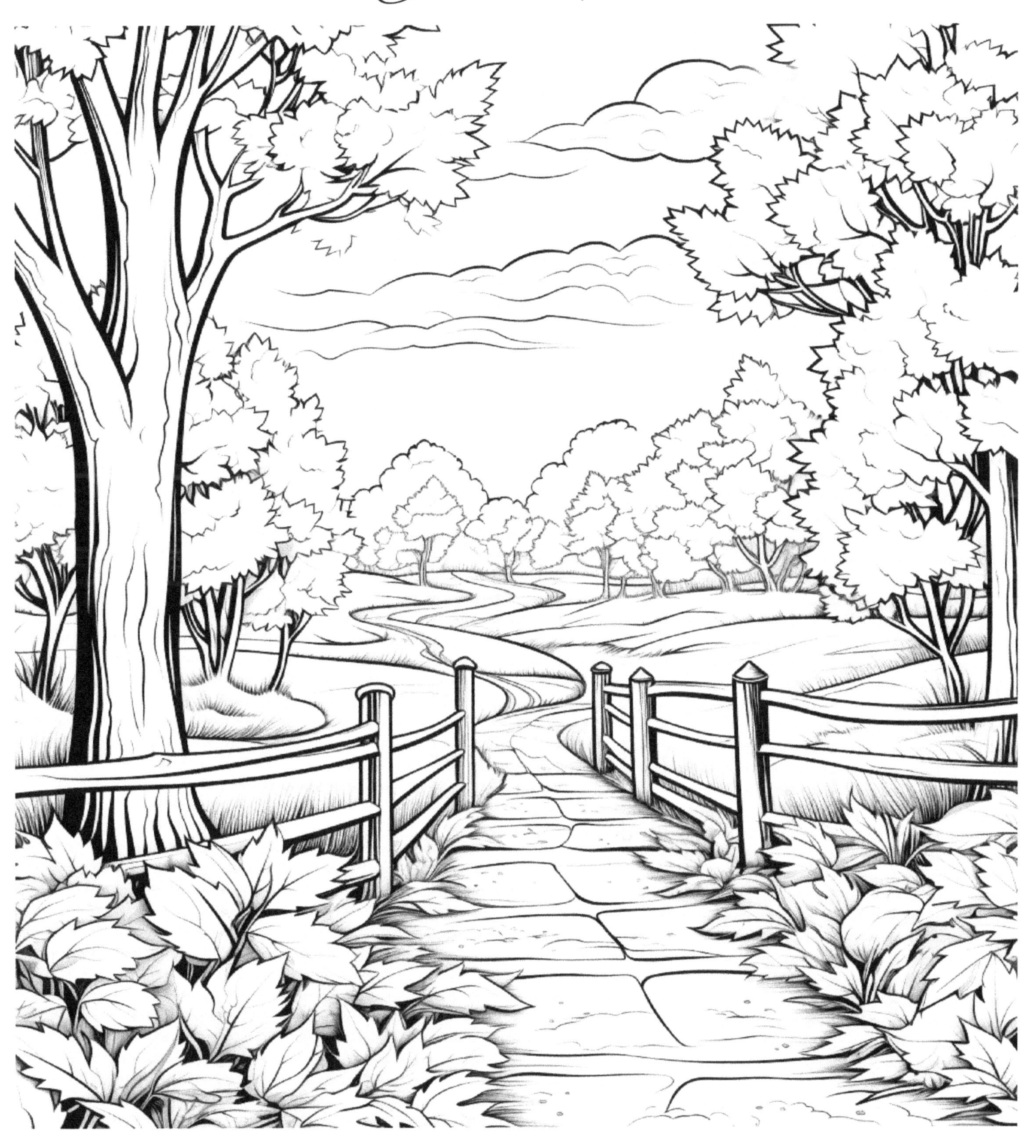

And My God Will Meet
All Your Needs In Christ
Pillippians 4:13

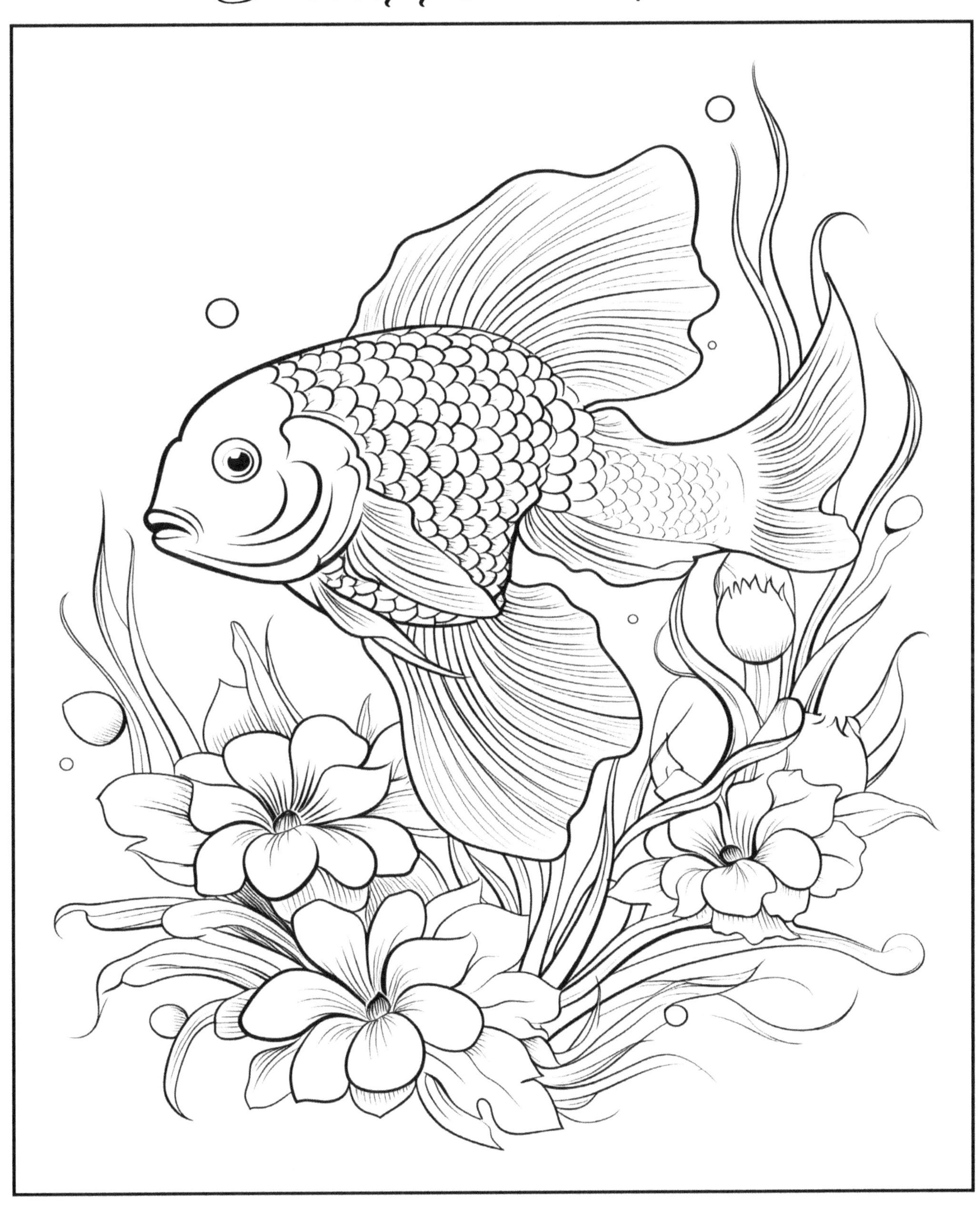

God Will Never Forget The Needy, The Hope Of The Afflicted Will Never Perish

Psalm 9:18

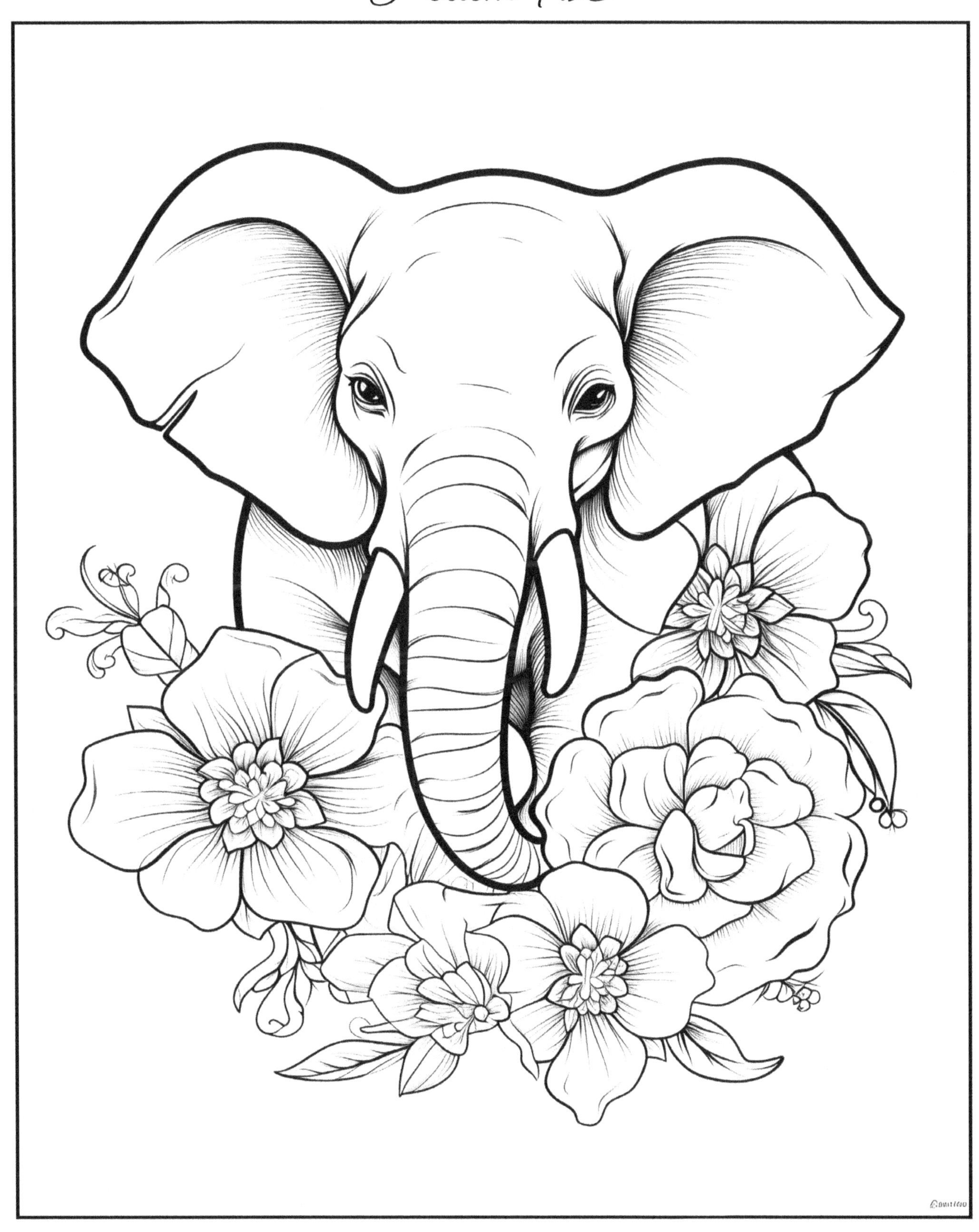

May The Lord Bless You And Keep You

Numbers 6:24

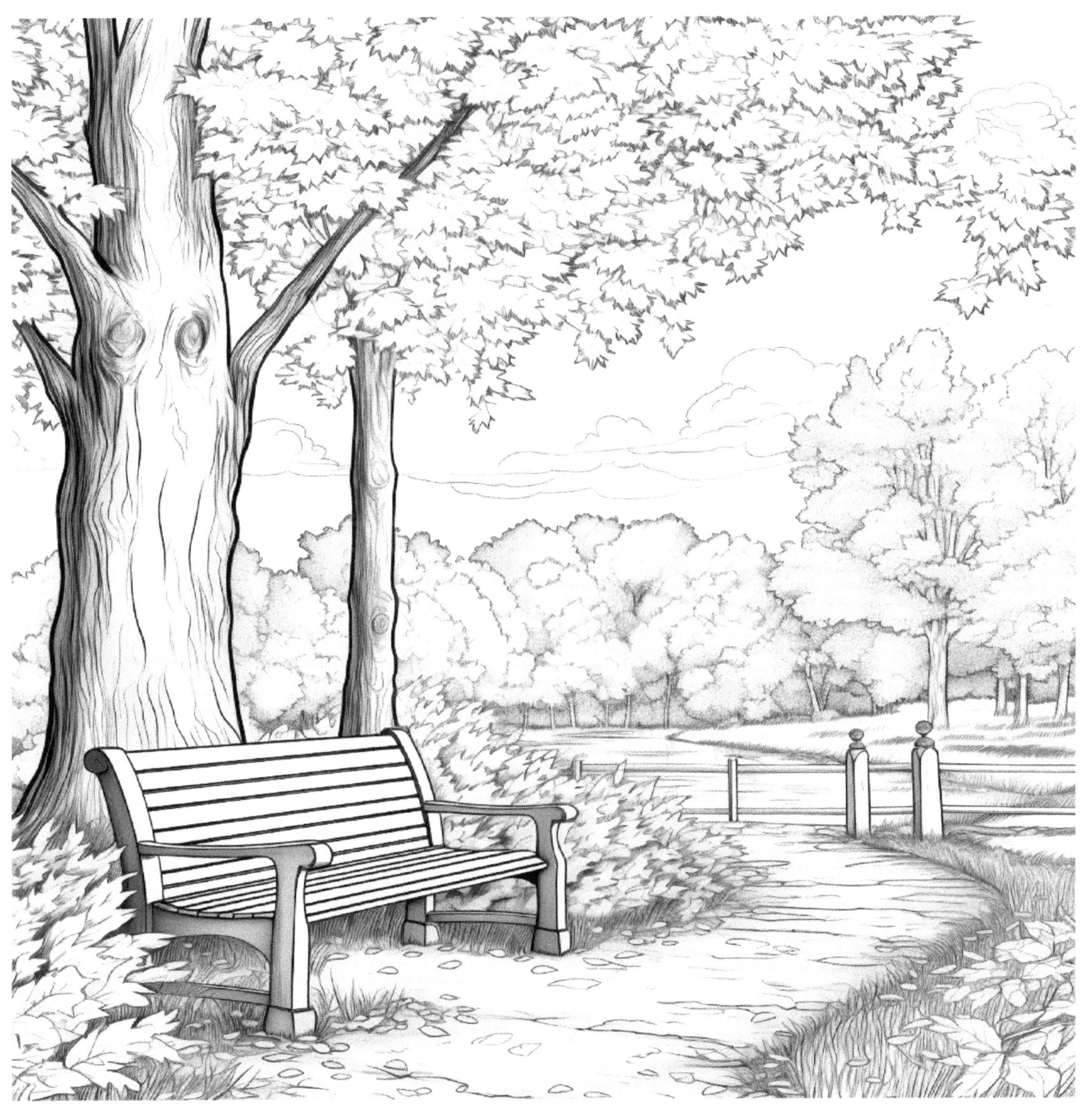

May The Lord Turn His Face Towards You And Give You Peace

Numbers 6:26

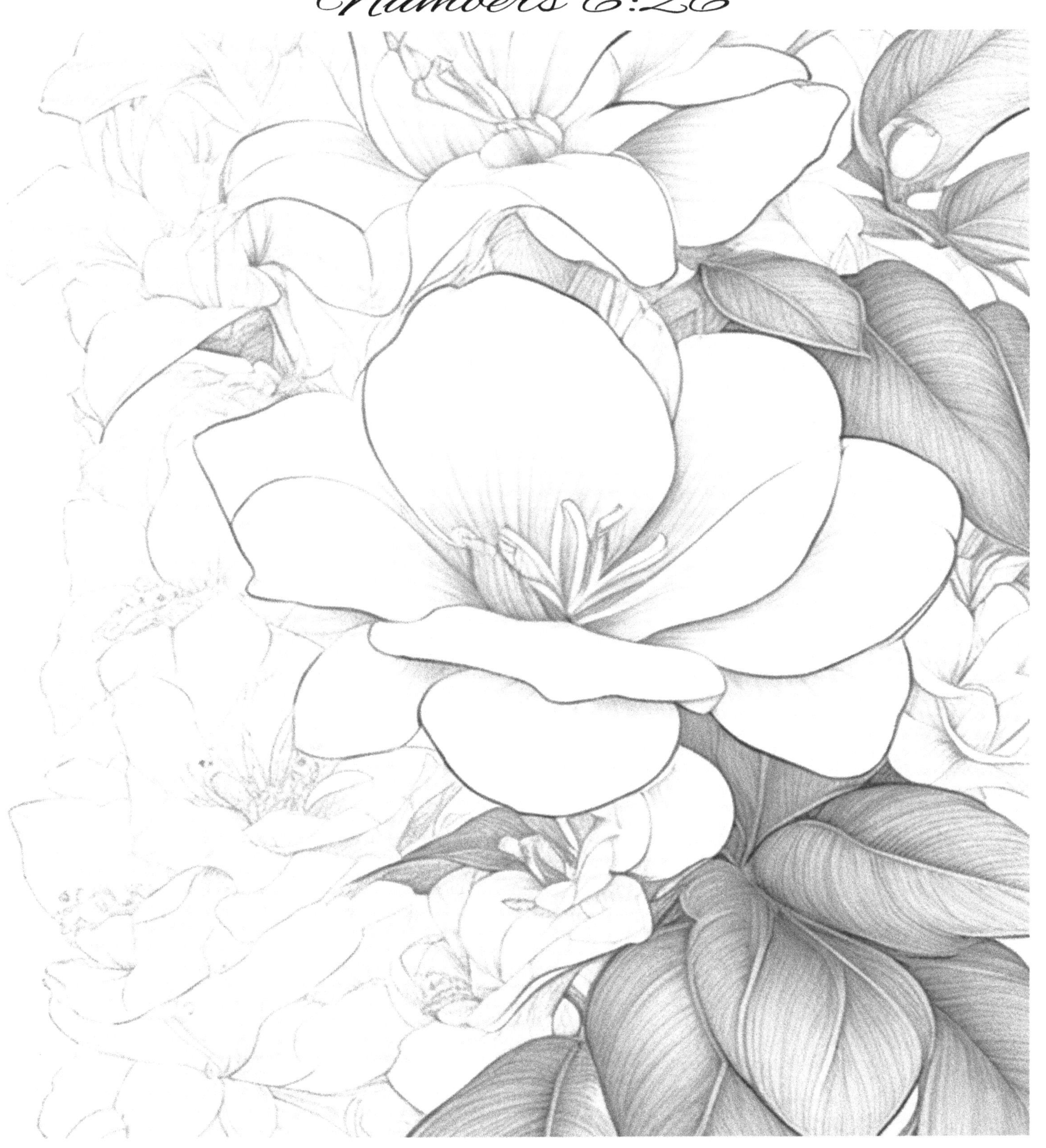

Nothing Will Be Able To Separate Us From The Love Of God In Jesus Christ

Romans 8:39

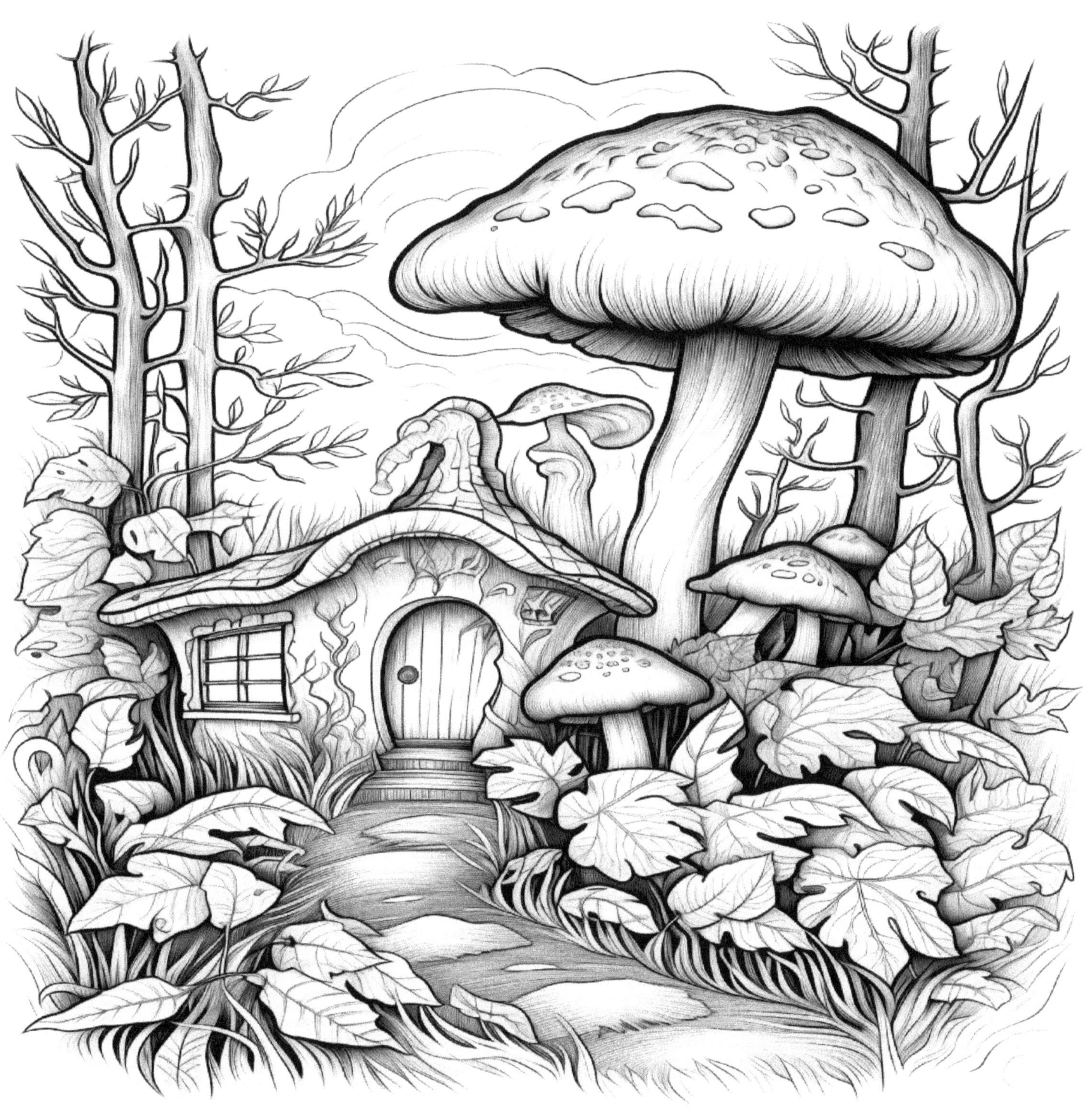

He Will Be Like A Tree, Firmly Planted By Streams Of Water

Psalm 1:3

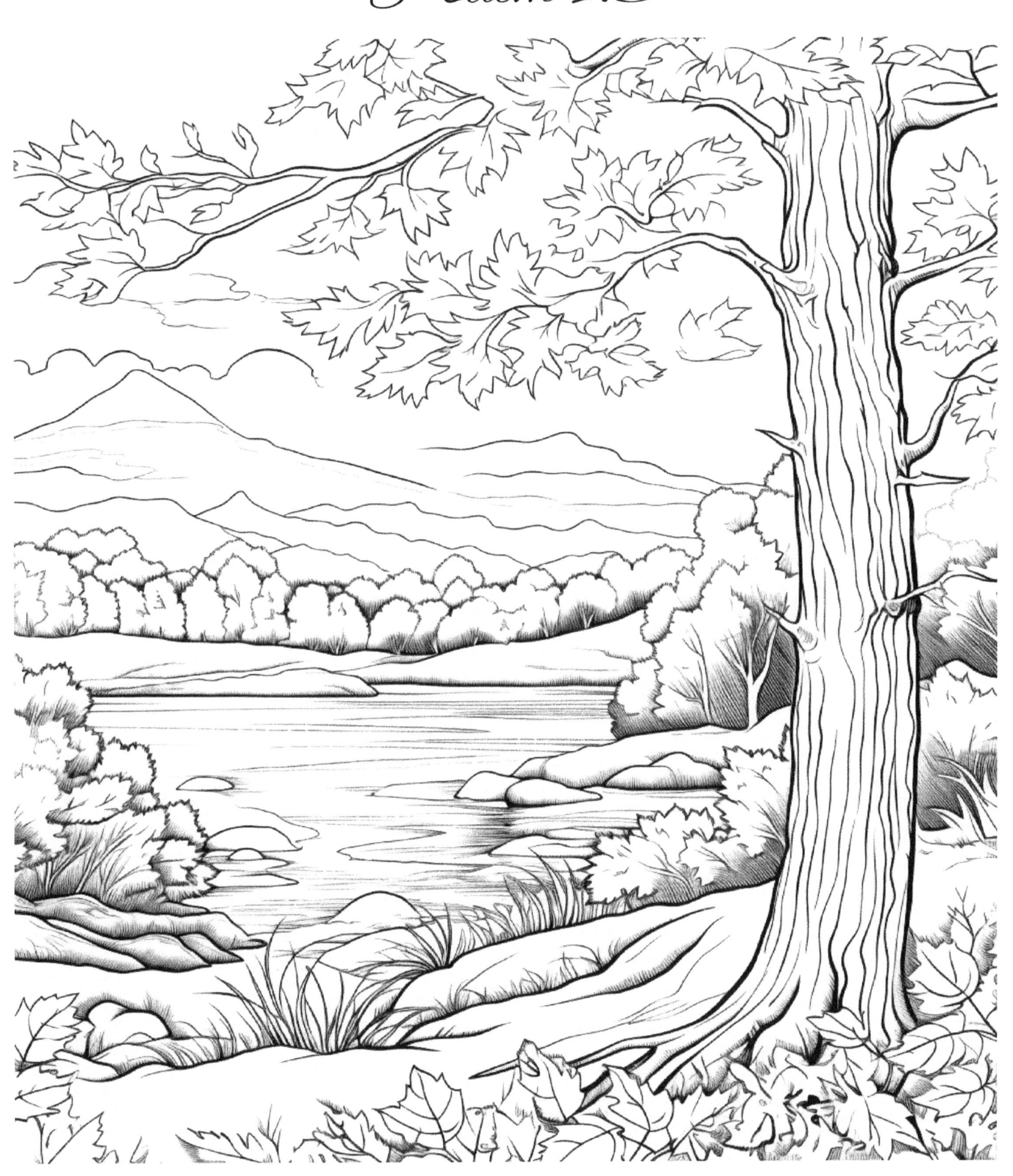

All Things Are Possible For One Who Believes

Mark 9:23

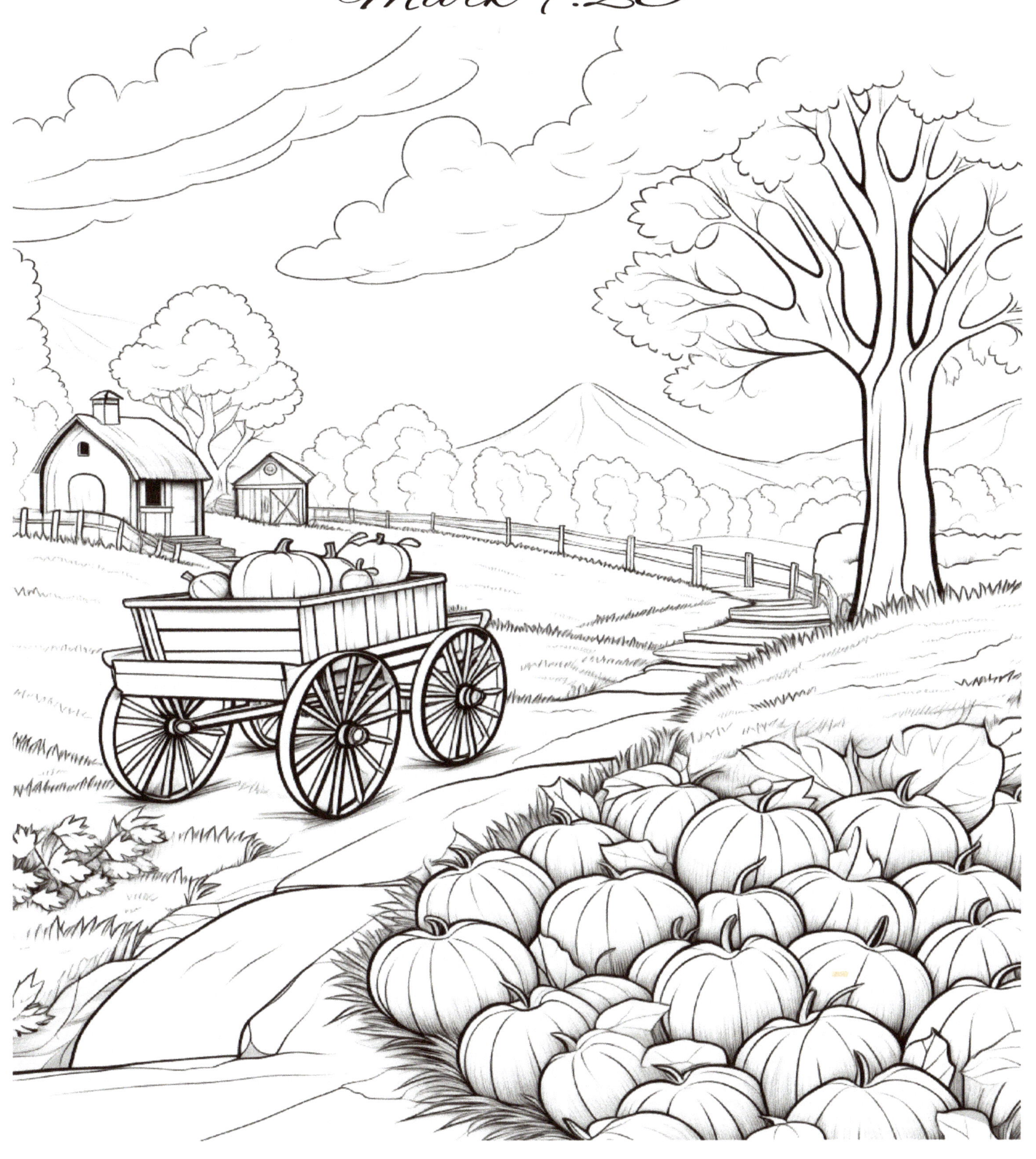

Even Though I Walk Through The Darkest Valley, I Will Fear No Evil For You Are With Me

Psalm 23:4

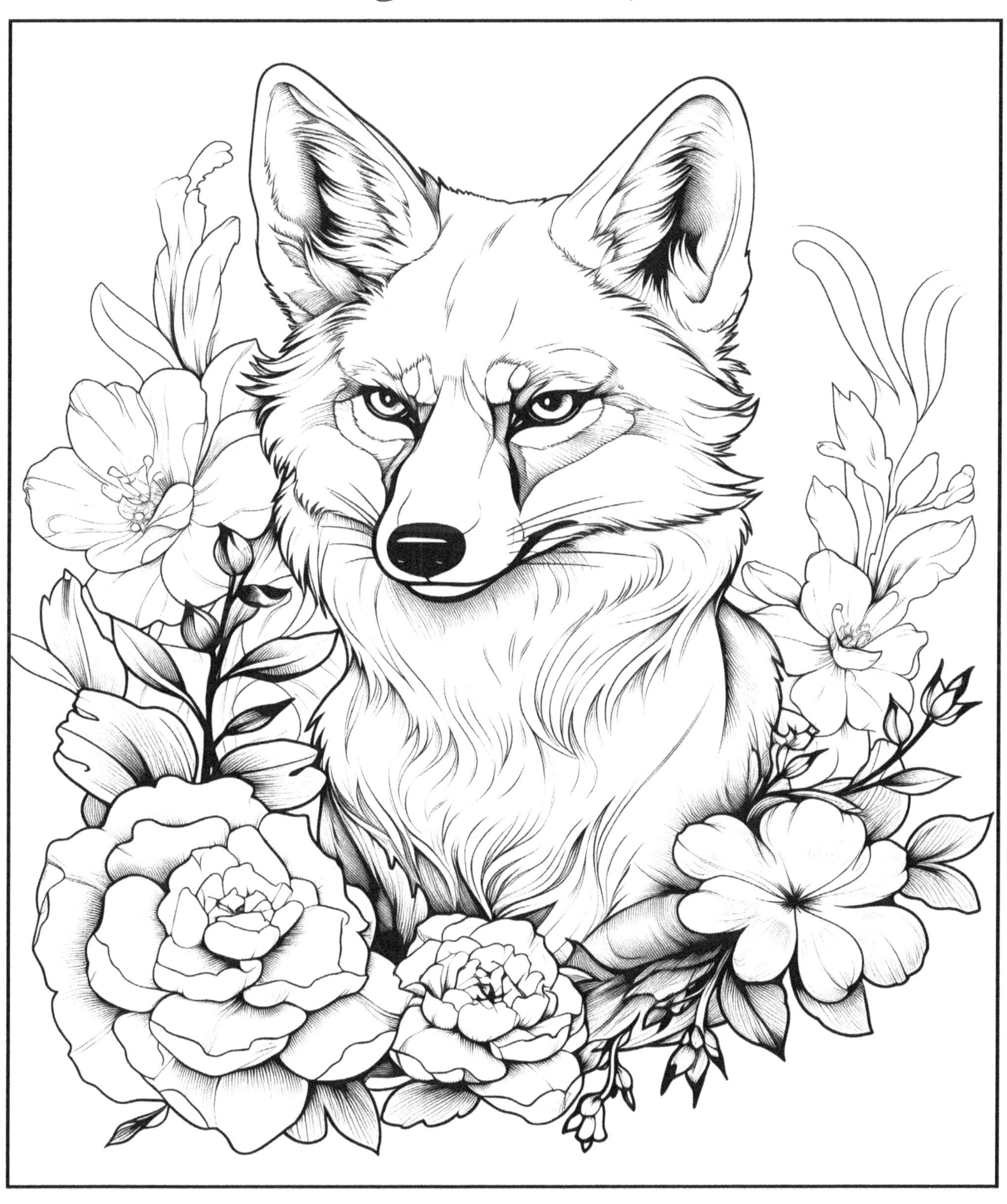

Can Anyone, By Worrying Add A Single Hour To Their Life?

Matthew 6:27

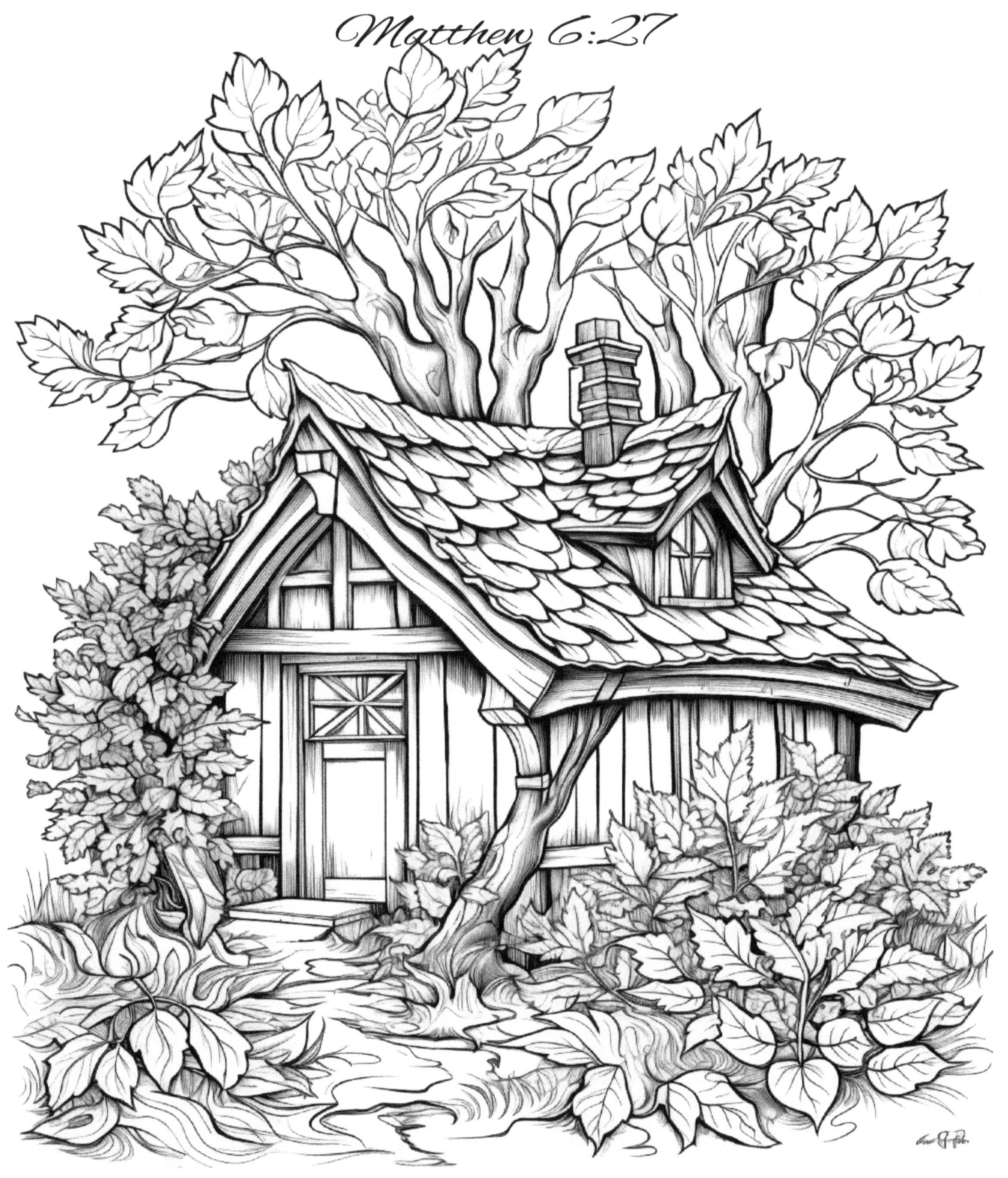

For God So Loved The World That He Gave His Only Begotten Son, That Whosoever Believes In Him Shall Not Perish

John 3:16

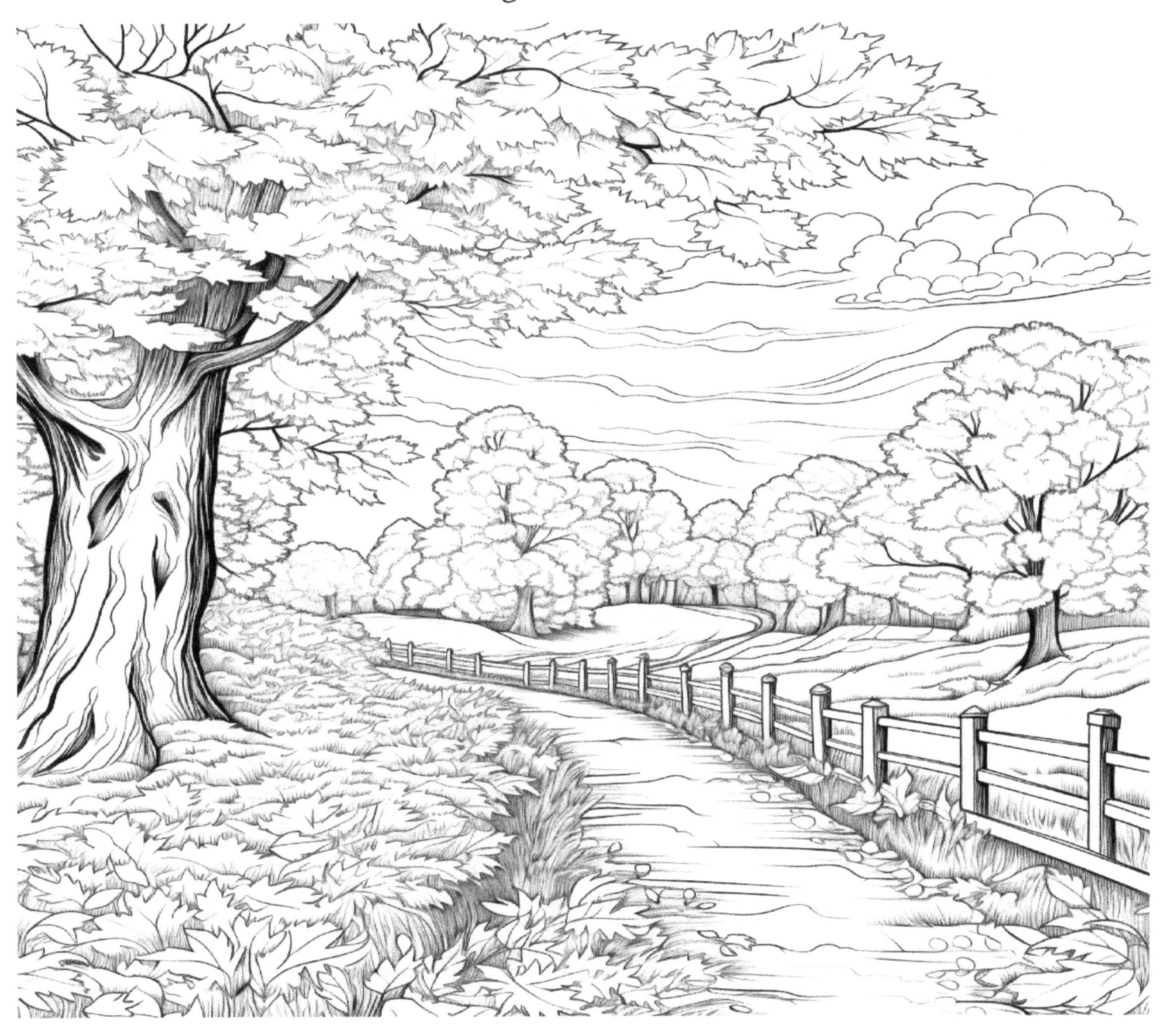